# The Palmetto State House

AMANDA CAUGHMAN DERRICK

*The Palmetto State House*

Copyright © 2021 by Amanda Caughman Derrick

First Edition

Paperback ISBN: 978-1-64990-458-4

# DEDICATION

For teachers and students
across the Palmetto State

In the center of South Carolina lies its capital city, Columbia. Columbia is home to South Carolina's State House.

This is a place that is rich in history and has many stories to share and tell.

The first capital of South Carolina was located in Charleston in the 1750s. It was a wooden structure and served our state well until leaders decided it was time to move our capital to the center of our state. South Carolina was growing, and people were moving to all parts of our state. Columbia was our nation's first planned capital city.

Moving the capital to Columbia made it easier for all people in South Carolina to get there.

The new State House was a wooden building next to where

the present-day State House is located. Members of our

government started meeting in Columbia in 1790.

Tension from the Civil War began to rise in the 1860s.

General William Sherman and his troops marched through

the midlands of our state, destroying homes, buildings, and

property in 1865.

Sherman and his men fired cannonballs from their cannons

across the Congaree River. The cannonballs hit the wooden

State House, and it burned to the ground.

The present-day State House was being built during this time period. Cannonballs struck this new structure, but it did not burn down.

Today, bronze stars mark the spots on the exterior of the building where the cannonballs hit.

The State House is made of our state rock, granite. The first piece of granite for our present-day State House was laid on April 21, 1855. It was mined in a quarry in Cayce, not far from the State House.

Our State House houses our state government. Inside the

State House, you will find our governor's office as well as

the lieutenant governor's office. They make up the executive

branch of our government. They make sure the laws of our

state are carried out.

The State House is also the place where our legislative branch meets to make the laws for our state. The two parts of this branch of government are the Senate and House of Representatives. There are forty-six senators who meet in the Senate chamber. The legislators, who number 124, meet in the House chamber. A *chamber* is another word for a large room.

The judicial branch is our state's court system. Each of our forty-six counties also has a judicial system. These groups of people make sure our state has laws that are fair to all of our citizens.

On the very top of our State House is a copper dome.

Which of our coins is made of copper? The penny is made

of copper. If you covered the State House dome with

pennies, it would take approximately 13,200,000 pennies

to cover this dome.

Atop the dome fly the American flag and the South

Carolina flag.

Our State House is an important building where South

Carolinians come together to work for the people of

our state.

They work to make South Carolina the best it can be.

CPSIA information can be obtained
at www.ICGtesting.com
Printed in the USA
LVHW070159210721
693272LV00001B/31